OFF TO SPACE!

THE MOON

by J. P. Press

Consultant: Beth Gambro
Reading Specialist, Yorkville, Illinois

Minneapolis, Minnesota

Teaching Tips

Before Reading

- Look at the cover of the book. Discuss the picture and the title.
- Ask readers to brainstorm a list of what they already know about the moon. What can they expect to see in this book?
- Go on a picture walk, looking through the pictures to discuss vocabulary and make predictions about the text.

During Reading

- Read for purpose. Encourage readers to think about the moon and the role it plays with Earth and space as they are reading.
- If readers encounter an unknown word, ask them to look at the sounds in the word. Then, ask them to look at the rest of the page. Are there any clues to help them understand?

After Reading

- Encourage readers to pick a buddy and reread the book together.
- Find a place in the book that tells about the moon and the sun. Find a page that tells about the moon and Earth.
- Ask readers to write a sentence and draw a picture of something that they learned about the moon.

Credits:
Cover and title page, © taffpixture/Shutterstock; 5, © JacquesKloppers/iStock; 7, © Igor Filonenko/Shutterstock and © Castleski/Shutterstock; 8–9, © Tristan3D/Shutterstock; 10, © chrisp0/iStock; 11, © kdshutterman/Shutterstock; 13, © taffpixture/Shutterstock; 14, © Cherdchai charasri/Shutterstock and © Vydrin/Shutterstock; 15, © pjmorley/iStock; 17, © NASA/JSC; 18, © Castleski/Shutterstock; 21, © Image Source/Alamy Stock Photo; 22, © Just Super/Shutterstock and © Wikimedia Commons/NASA; 23BL, © Tristan3D/Shutterstock; 23BR, © georgeclerk/iStock; 23TL, © Voraorn Ratanakorn/Shutterstock; 23TR, © IVAN ABORNEV/Shutterstock

Library of Congress Cataloging-in-Publication Data

Names: Press, J. P., 1993– author.
Title: The moon / J.P. Press ; consultant, Beth Gambro.
Description: Minneapolis, Minnesota : Bearport Publishing Company, [2021] |
   Series: Off to space! | Includes bibliographical references and index.
Identifiers: LCCN 2020030831 (print) | LCCN 2020030832 (ebook) | ISBN
   9781647475062 (library binding) | ISBN 9781647475116 (paperback) | ISBN
   9781647475161 (ebook)
Subjects: LCSH: Moon—Juvenile literature.
Classification: LCC QB582 .P747 2021 (print) | LCC QB582 (ebook) | DDC
   523.3—dc23
LC record available at https://lccn.loc.gov/2020030831
LC ebook record available at https://lccn.loc.gov/2020030832

Copyright © 2021 Bearport Publishing Company. All rights reserved. No part of this publication may be reproduced in whole or in part, stored in any retrieval system, or transmitted in any form or by any means, electronic, mechanical, photocopying, recording, or otherwise, without written permission from the publisher.

For more information, write to Bearport Publishing, 5357 Penn Avenue South, Minneapolis, MN 55419.

Printed in the United States of America.

Contents

Look at the Moon! 4

Fun Moon Facts 22

Glossary 23

Index 24

Read More 24

Learn More Online 24

About the Author 24

Look at the Moon!

The night is dark.

But look up at the sky and see light.

The moon is **bright** tonight.

Where does the moon's light come from?

It comes from the sun!

The sun shines light on the moon.

The moon is always on the move!

It **travels** around Earth.

The path it takes is called its **orbit**.

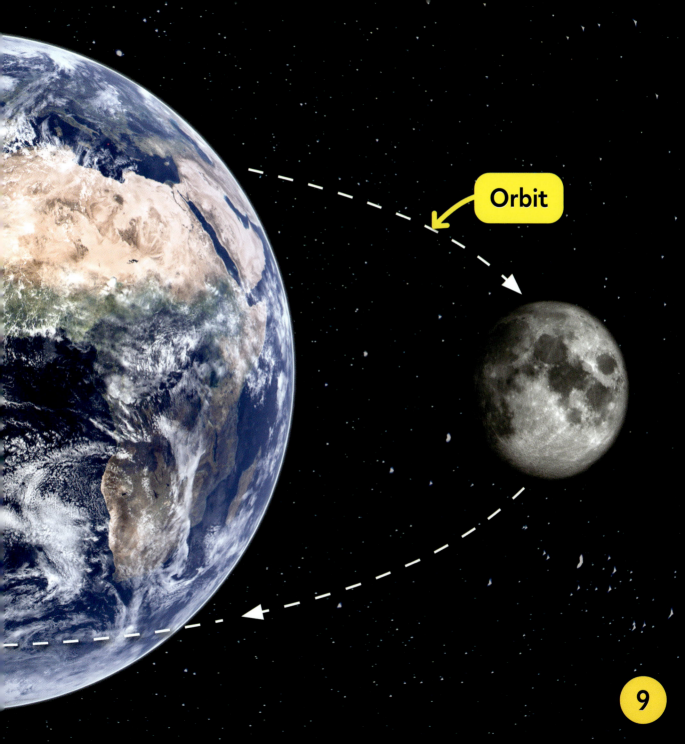

Some days, the moon is thin.

Other days, the moon looks like a big ball.

How can that be?

We see only the moon where it gets light.

Sometimes lots of light gets to the moon.

Sometimes very little light gets there.

13

Earth is bigger than the moon.

Think of Earth as the size of a basketball.

Then, the moon is the size of a tennis ball.

15

The moon is made of rock.

Gray rocks and gray dust cover the moon.

The moon has tall **mountains**.

It has big holes, too.

17

Do you want to take a trip to the moon?

Some people have!

In 1969, the first person walked on the moon.

His name was Neil.

After that, 12 more people walked on the moon.

Maybe you will go to the moon someday, too!

Fun Moon Facts

More than 400 tree seeds from Earth went to the moon. They were planted on Earth after they came back from space. They are called Moon Trees!

A Moon Tree

The moon looks a lot like a ball. But it is really shaped a bit like an egg.

More than 100 robots have been on the moon. Many are still there!

Glossary

bright giving off or filled with lots of light

mountains areas of land that rise very high above the land around them

orbit the path of an object that is circling a planet or the sun

travels moves from one place to another

23

Index

Earth 8, 14, 22
light 4, 6, 12
mountains 16
orbit 8–9
rock 16
sun 6–7

Read More

Moon, Walt K. *Let's Explore the Moon (A First Look at Space).* Minneapolis: Lerner Publications, 2018.

Rector, Rebecca Kraft. *The Moon.* New York: Enslow, 2019.

Learn More Online

1. Go to **www.factsurfer.com**
2. Enter "**Space Moon**" into the search box.
3. Click on the cover of this book to see a list of websites.

About the Author

J. P. Press has an uncle that helped us look at space. This is for Michael.